the window of a sandcastle

poems

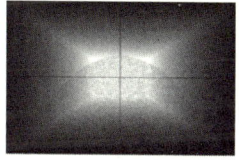

amu nnadi

origami

ISBN: 978-31574-4-2

National Library of Nigeria
Cataloguing-in-Publication Data

Published in Nigeria by:

Parresia Publishers Ltd.
Under its Origami Books Imprint
9, Oluwole Close, Okota, Lagos,
Nigeria

www.parresia.com.ng

through the
window of
a sandcastle

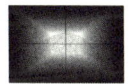

Jamila Mimi

amu nnadi

origami

Also by amu nnadi

the fire within
pilgrim s passage

our lives are a
seamless stream
of many commas
but no stops

Thanks to

Timi Alaibe
without question

Anietie Okon
father

Lambert Konboye
a poet's friend

Also
Uzor Maxim Uzoatu
Richard Ali...
belief gives spirit to the word

For

Okechi Amu-Nnadi

&

Alaere Alaibe

you wrote the finest poem with your lives

contents

xi

in the beginning was the word...
all things were made by the word
and without the word was not anything made
that was made

the word is life
life never ends

...

the word inhabits the poem
the poem inhabits the man
through the poem the word lives
through the word the world lives

as the poet writes,
life is a seamless stream
of many commas
but no stops

so are we

we cannot die

period

Poetry, oh poetry
Just as Jesus is the lily of the valley
Poetry is the tree of life
Like the lights of New York city
It lights the way for others.

Oh poetry
It does not have to rhyme
Even do you think so
It is so simple
Just arrange meaningful words and lines
To a paragraph

I love poetry
Because it is not just a thing
It is a way of life

'Gozira Amu-Nnadi (7)
for Chijioke

wreaths

okechi

sometimes i think
the things beautiful and strong about me
are constantly being swept away
now they fly away
now they fall about the grey tombstones
of my autumn
falling

arlington

autumn grows old on me
weary leaves, cold sidewalks
and creaky trees leaning on bent canes
i grow old with it, weary from running mile
after mile, my head crowned
with its changing hairs like
this city

the chill clasps mean fingers round my throat
the only drink i offer arlington, brutal host
with scarce a smile, i have
nothing to smile about, so i stare back
tears forming, heart unfeeling, hands
stuck deep into deeper pockets
where the last coins tell you
how far from home you are

it is strange how sometimes you cry
without feeling
like meat thawing, losing arrogance
benumbed more from fears of the unknown
than these stark reminders that slowly,
inevitably,
everything finds its way home

you think of home when everything is strangely
suffocating, when duvets are not enough
you think of growing old
when all around you leaves brown, trees
undress, reveal bare essentials,
grey mourning grey mornings reveal
as we inch slowly, slowly
to our destination

home comes soon enough for those
who grow old, grow weary

from all the miles run, naked from
all the leaves shed, trees
that drop their weary souls on you,
awaiting the rebirth of a season, awaiting
a new place

home comes soon enough
for those who grow old

nakedness

it is the nakedness of autumn
i have come to know
trees stuck in their ways
just like me
shed their innocence into piles of refuse
for the world around me is built
on wasted things
dreams, childhood,
and fire that goes out in the eye
when the sun sinks in our horizon

i stand naked like autumn
it is so much like me
set in my ways
and bereft of dreams, bereft
of fire, damp
so damp like soiled napkins

i am surrounded by dust
and swirling wind
smell of leaves dying
anguish of exposed branches
thin, gnarled fingers
despairing at exposed clouds
arthritic
poking

i am surrounded by dying things
winds gurgling through slit throats,
protesting
clouds exposing famished thighs,
drifting into sin
gay cobwebs dancing,
trapping dreams
beauty shed into piles of refuse
to be raked into merry bundles of dead dreams

and swept away

birds duck to other climes
fleeing
fleeing

sometimes i think
things beautiful and strong about me
are constantly being swept away
now they fly away
now they fall about the grey tombstones
of my autumn
falling
falling

i am stuck in my ways, i say
unless i learn to move
soon
they will sweep me away

bitterness

in its bitterest form
anguish stalks white of clouds, darkly
forming tears waiting to be shed
bitter, bitter rain soaks my earth
flood i run with, flotsam, debris and all

too overcome,
i am unable to stand
and take in a breath

i am raining again
dry, it comes against season
comes with air too tormented
it bathes everything
and bitter, i knot myself like pain
to reconcile this shadow with my soul

everything comes dark and unlovely
even the light of your countenance
the smile that plays around those thin lips
accusing
condemning

you turn away smiling again, my soul
and i bitterly
to the darkness and laughter in the air

in its bitterest form
melancholy comes in tattered clothes
revealing
pun
     ctuating
edges frayed
threads of our lives hanging loose
holding nothing

how many times you turn away, my soul
bare almost
devoid of intensities
stranger i court with confusion and love
fear i make my bed with
soft pillow of dark, dark clouds

i hear again the soul speak
with strange, strangled voices
a chatter of rain torments my earth
it soaks everything
repeats with groans her vain reassurances

yet i am dry
so dry
tattered and bare

golgotha

i crouch in the dark
my soul, my face
all that become me
i am nothing
just this rain hooded night
awaiting sparks of life

i am surrounded by skulls
on golgotha
the mirthless sky cracks her whip
eyes flashing, tongue flicking
it snakes across my country
illuminating dead heirs to a promise

it presages the death that comes
fangs, a bite, venom and all

here on this darkened hill
i stand, eyes gouged out
it is only darkness i see
no moon to light my path
no tears to water me
and make me sprout

rod of moses in hand
i stumble after shadows
flanked by thieves,
an owl sees deeper than night
its call a lament through sharpened lips
hard, brutal to the point

shapes of defiant trees
rooted to their many fanged pride
beckon
they search out my dishevelled soul
their branches flog me

they draw blood
sweet jesus, they draw blood
and peter squats before bonfires
of my heart
an ancient lie on his lips

hoping to unburden me
i cut me into pieces
of broken hearts
hoping to bleed, hoping to be
hoping my blood irrigates this land

hoping
my death is not in vain

old dreams

i wake up to those old dreams
with their flaming eyes and
bloodstained teeth
they reach out like spears, stabbing
my heart bleeds from wounds of
uncharted shores
bearing my river like pharaoh's nile

i break a bread of bricks
chewing slowly, it disintegrates into dust
fills my mouth, fills
my heart with brittle bits of dreams

is it my anger
is it my dread
is this my shadow
casting darkness across my heart

who am i? who am i? who am i? my soul chants
there are red seas to cross
rocks to bring to tears with a whip
a poem to write with a staff
and i don't have a clue

i mount a chariot of familiar fears
without a wish
i grate my substance against your denials
waters close up around me
laughing
slapping
spitting salt into my eyes

who am i? who am i? who the heck
am i? my heart beats
am i rooted to a spot?
am i flying away?

do i have a shadow?
who the heck am i?

once i was an animal
tethered to a point
once i was a flaming tree
standing on a spot
once i was a wall of feuding water
rising into waves of despair
once i was a world of toads
breaking into a dirge

once i was a small still lament
once i was a sea of blood
once i was darkness
once i wore a crown of thorns
nailed to a cross

once i was, once i was
my soul chants
now i am lost

some things never change
my songs and their piercing thorns
they spear, stabbing
cutting me to pieces

broken

walls sprout across me
it is jericho once more
and i can't scream enough

they say i am possessed
by all my possessions
half truth, half spirit
i am my own worst fear
and my cry is of things
high walled and prepossessing

i sit on my saddle
going round and round
the bend
looking for your under belly, lord
trumpet in hand

hungers lead me on
i come upon a jaded jordan
finding no life i lie upon the waters
i climb a tree, holding on like leaves
it is your wall, high and insurmountable

i embrace you to find canaan
you are a fence of cactus
i sit upon your back, feet astride
crying
reaching
falling

why can't i hold on to you
why can't i hold you
why can't i speak your tongue
why can't i break you down
seeing as i blow atop my lungs

why can't you hold me to your breast
and taste the bile in my breath
why can't you see the tears in my eyes
growing into this river of darkness

i blow hard lord, too hard perhaps
cracks show on my trumpet
cracks on my walls
i fall, again, broken
like a vase

ashes

i kick up ashes
looking for that last stubborn flame
it hides beneath waste
beneath memories of what we have shared
and killed
it flares at the air
exposed as nostrils
splutters and dies

the ash on my feet is fitting
we mark ourselves
with ghosts of our feasts

for
everything goes to waste
everything dies
everything is buried beneath
the ash of moonlight
and all we do is kick
kick and raise nothing
but dust

everything becomes dust
even our last stubborn flame

why should i care

why should i care if flowers die
if their soft petals turn lip up
heartbroken, sombre like dirt
and slowly brown, disintegrate
and fall down to earth

why should i care if water loses its way
searching for its level
frightened, snapping like mongrels
ferrying waste and my drenched soul
swallowing bits of my earth

why should i care if the sun goes blind
returning home for dinner
groping, tapping its rays like a cane
and, lost, lies down among a shiver of rivers
dandruff of stars on hunched shoulder

why should i care if birds lose their feathers
neck bent to the pot in wordless plea
feet knotted, gripping nothing
but their pride
wishing futilely feathers hold up our head

why should i care if flowers die
if water loses its way
if the sun, gutted, goes blind

why should i, why should i care
if we go home hungry
if our head drops down
if life stares with gutted eyes
and there is nothing
but fallen flowers, broken earth
and graves of what is dreamed

on a spot

been standing on a spot
too confused to go forward
for the cyclone raises a bull temper
sets the bushes on fire

before me the fire speaks, eyes
aflame, and eats up my rivers
behind, swirling dust
covers my footprints
howling:
> you have no past to claim

our smoke drifts into heaven
our dust drifts into heaven
no rain, just a cascade of ash
falling upon our heads
as we march to occupy

it must be he sleeps
removed from our cosmos of dreams
it must be he sleepwalks
muttering:
> give them hell
> give them hell

what hell? this is hell

how can he not see the fire burning
how can he not hear our cries
how can he not see the charred bodies
laid out on a stone

i am standing on my spot
waiting for a sign
> of hope
either the fire reaches me
or dust swallows my name

haze

my view of you is distant
through this harmattan haze
a million grains mask your face
and we lose intimacy
i lose my hold of you
lose traction like an old tyre

we spin out of control
twister of dreams carrying dust
and debris of wasted years
this now is my lot with you
too many yarns spun, too many
heads lost to mindless, faceless
purloin of seasons

to reclaim you i spin my own tale
having lost my way
having lost you
in this gathering of dust

you were the girl of childhood
nights made intimate by silence
and the chirping of our hearts
our hop over gutters when we saw no waste
only a mirror of clapping stars
your eyes clear as water and hope
and i would hold your hand
and renew with you my vow of loyalty
and service

you were the young cashew trees
lined in military rows behind milliken hill
soft fruits ripe with promise
yellow without fear
i remember the juice dribbling messifully
down

stubborn stain on white
more kind than this stain upon the heart

you were always the coconut juice
sweeter than the hard nut
we must crack
thicker than tears

through your haze i reach out for grains
i find only husks, my land
only remains of harvests
only masks of forgotten years

and this brutal wall of dust

as clothes on a line

we are arrayed as clothes on a line
waiting to dry up, waiting
for our moment in the sun

above, clouds move as they do
moment to pregnant moment
filtering tides, swollen like bladder
with wasted pride

below, grasses, strangely held
to a point
            of view
stare skywards, hands raised to heaven
seeking a soul they find
only empty sleeves, empty pockets
emptiness where once our lives lived

wind comes searching, flies too
rifling through our beings
finding nothing they fill our lives
with air
our empty spaces with nothing
we can see

we sway from side to tide
harvested corn stalks
flap like clipped birds
stuck on worn lives
too empty to stand on a dream
and stare back with meaning

too frayed to stand strong
and dare the wind

our lives

you begin to fold your life like this
into balls of fufu
when there is nothing to do
but form a fist

everything is fondly soft
and joyous like a ball, full
of bounce and filled
with your very breath,
and this hunger
not to let life be too square

but to bite and hold on
is an illusion
to chew fills you
with a bland lack of soup
fills your akala aka with waste
and crusts of what our lives should be

wreaths

okechi

i lay wreaths on the tombstone of our life
it is all i do now
concussed by memory and many unfinished
poems
i write the twisted stem of loss
sad letters of shuffling leaves
blown hither, thither in a year

your hymns echo in my head
make my tongue heavy
blessed assurance, jesus is mine
not ours,
is not of hope but starvation
forgotten notes stalk my heart
tears escape like bats from one darkness
overshadowing another

leaves fall from grace
fall from sturdy branches of stunted hopes
fall from eyes, bitter and arid
and mark our lawns with dying promises
it is so finite, so total
foreboding
just like this

we mark our days with those leaves
bound together in the song of our lives
they brown, twisting
shrivelling
dying
just like this

every leaf broken dies
every stem broken dies
every fruit broken dies

every pen dries up
like ase, spring of childhood
and dies

but your hymn
stubborn and finite
lives
humming like my mind
with this

ihe juru onu

port harcourt rains wash away my face
they are more flood than tears
and i hold flotsam of shared moments
like a paddle
thinking, my father was more alive
than all the waters of rivers

i am stumped like the stump of
a fallen tree
and all the remains of our years
all our lives gather round me
filtering tears, wailings
and many unspoken tributes

openings jump into my gecko head
i cannot wrap myself around them
seeing i dangle from a balcony
simple words evade me
as meteors a darkening sky
verses evade my universe

i cannot give you father
ozo okechi amu nnadi
ihe juru onu adigi ntagbute
nna chiri nweze
nwa eze oha ogota elemu
a fitting goodbye

you are too tall, too rich
you are all the palms of the world
you fill my mouth, tough roasted meat
you fill my cry

you are an elephant
you are a house
i bite into you in vain
igwurube oru miiii

i cannot hold all of you

a star, i cannot leave your sky
a fish, i cannot leave your river
a tree, i cannot leave your soil
a bird, i cannot fly and not return
to your nest, nwa eze oha ogota

you are all the stars
you are all the rivers
you are all the dunes, hunchbacked and resolute
you gather all the grains of life
and all the floods cannot wash you away
all the words cannot hold you

you are eternal my father
one cannot put eternity in a simple word
one cannot mesmerise the stars with a simple smile
a cloud cannot hold on to tears
a house cannot hold a flood
igara cannot hold all the words of grief
odo achi knows all the secrets of life

okechi amu nnadi
nna chiri nweze
igwurube oru miiii
nwa eze oha ogota
my goodbye returns to me
my mouth floods with words of grief
and i cannot chew you

ihe juru onu
you are all the words of life
you are all the words of life, my father
ihe juru onu na adigi ntagbute
okechi amu nnadi
nwa eze oha ogota elemu
you are all the words of life

alaere

your memory follows me
not like the shadow i see
dark and patterned after my form
and sorrow
but the throbbing that imbues my heart
with a groan

each beat repeats your departure
repeats each leaf that leaves a branch
withers and dies
among clumps of loosened earth

you are the air i encounter everywhere
fresh here
odorous there
yet from which i draw in the life
that forms us

        you are constant as statue
        relentless as life
        resolute as death

slowly we chew your morsel
your tales of clear streams
and smile of flashing light
your eyes, calm as cheese
light as air

life is bitter
        leaf
edible only because we squeeze it
        to death
no juice, no substance
just twisted bits of a brief season
and wisps of what could have been

grief marches across our heart
a column of fevered ants
it climbs into the eyes
with its many stinging feet
reaches higher than trees, deeper
than a solitary grave in trofani

you fly away as the eagle, great one
as always you were, as you are
thick plumed, taloned grace
filled with undiminishable light
filled with an unending song
free
free

you leave us, alaere
with our faces to the sun
we stare into eternity
follow the tail of your burnished light
your star that inhabits the darkened skies
above our heads

we reach out to touch the stars
to hold on to your light
we are too little, inhabited by
brittle branches, nebulous nests
and wailing owls

we wither and die

zizi

unfinished

i
i saw you zizi
and you broke my heart
you were black in places
in most parts
your skin, tender and warm still
was doused in hot oil
red like grief

yet you were me
dark with that faint hint of milk
your hair, soft and coiled like music notes
were me
your nails were me
your nose was me
and in your tiny veins
my warm blood ran cold
stood still
stilled by the icy grip of death

you were peaceful, zizi
and in your peace
i stood dead

ii
i tried speaking to you
words would not come
they were the clot of blood
in your mother's throat
coming up from the deep

she has been coming up since
choking on your name

ah zizi

i speak to you still
with lumps of my grief

i speak and you become
silence
become the silence of
the hunter of preys
on the savannah of my sorrow

iii
we named you zizi
the full meaning
is meaningless now
yet how fitting
zizi is zzzzzz

how you sleep in the
depths
swallowed
how you swallow your name
unawakened

did i kill you with a name
did i name you with sleep
lifelong and unending
did death hide in the pouch
of your name
fire and brand at hand

i speak your name
i hear echoes of silence
the solemn purity of chancels
and mutters of unuttered
sermons

zizi
how i speak your name
with reverence

pilgrim before a cruel plain
bowed by the malevolence of
angry winds
bleached by angry suns

how i fear the malevolence
of death

iv
yet you were life
you were the tiny bulges
and steady kicks we laughed over
your mother and i

you were her breathlessness
and discomfort
the swell of her nose
the cramps and the pain

you were our expectations
and hopes
the new warm clothes
and huggies
which remain unwrapped
in a cold cot
just like your name

ah zizi
you were the white lines and ash
on a certain cold monitor
inbetween grey skeletons of life
how hard you kicked that monday night
your heart pumping like pistons
of a journey

my heart pumping too
with the journeys we would take
the suns we would tame

racing like wild winds
which stop now
tamed, before a ravine
and tumble into the void

v
ah zizi
you were life
undefined

a hint
a tease
foretaste
shadows and smoke
mournful music notes
mocking the altars of life

vi
you cannot be this death
that is so stark
this white sheet
in which they wrapped you
like a message
stamped undelivered
backtosender

vii
i have been writing for a while now
yet the clock says the same thing
quarter to twelve
everything stands still, zizi
stands still
while you inspect our parade
of life
and float away

life stands still
still

viii
i think i am dreaming
i think i am suspended
to a point
i think i am
i think i
i think
i thin
i
not getting to the end
not knowing the finality
of twelve

zizi
dear daughter i named
how so much like life you are
how so much like death you become

somewhere they will find a grave for you

somewhere they will find a grave for you, son

i have written the last dirge
all the words have left me
emptied of light like a childless night
now i laugh at life
carefree like the wind, going here and there
neither here nor there

be gone, little one
you have chosen your path
and your path is not with me
you are not with me
you have chosen a path with the wind

perhaps you will see the others gone before
zizi and the other without a name
dark spots where my stars flamed out
i too may not be too far behind
for life has a bad attitude
it goes where and when it chooses

too untamed, i cannot call it my own
too impatient, it goes where and when it chooses
neither here nor there
just like you
just like all of you

somewhere they will find a grave for you too
as life does for us all

drags

anna nicole smith

you dragged in your world in one fell sniff
intoxicating, it becomes a haunting firelight
of sparks, sprouted horns and screams
that were in your ears music
and in your eyes fumes of dreams

and i say, party 💃
that is why your world was rocky
your heart a salon of wanton heat
only you could tell
with that red-lipped pout

you danced to every song
and wore life like bikini
hiding nothing, revealing a tormented soul
you popped pills in thrills
and dared disaster in dating

you wooed life with octogenarian dust
and found husband in grandfather,
you pursued a father in nothing but
drifting shadows of tales and smoke
and now it all slips through your hourglass waist
slipping with you

no wonder that morning with larry king
carrying your innocence like a burden of life
and bitterness
a shadow passedover your lovely eyes
into darkness

shadows were always your rite of passage
your firelight
for you trapped life
into a

brittle
emaciated
forlorn
longing

you dragged your world in, raindrenched cat
and hid your substance in a hole in our earth
you wore life like a hat
so sharpedged, like damocles' sword
you thought it a crown
now it falls upon you
it falls upon you, anna,
without mercy

and now
grains of regrets in my mouth
i offer you this handful of ash
and dust
for when you follow dust, anna
you become nothing but dust, ash
and brittle bits of a breath less earth

dust

you wonder why i am so dry
and blow about weightless
cobwebs stranded in stale air
among withered branches
without substance

you wonder why
i am the colour of dirt
earth of swept dreams
awaiting rain
upon a clenched hill

i am no more than dust
settling on leaves
after a storm
i am no more than
this dust upon your feet

wipe me off
and walk

through the window of a sandcastle

the wind says many things:

        rivers grow many nipples
        as they dance

        reeds, slim and gullible as a girl
        giggle as you tickle, bending
        by the waist

        coconut trees are fertile with many testicles
        here in badagry, they bear many sons
        and bury some in the sand

there are many paths to a river
marked by where our feet buried our souls
they gather waters of our lives
and grow deep in grim memorials

across paths skeletons crisscross
        in medieval meditation
the wind speaks with astringent tongue
asking, why is the heart of crabs
        all soft and tender
why must we break bones
        to find the marrow of a man

there, where waterweed fix eyelashes
to a dirty road, wary of saltwater
a lone egret stands, peering into the sun
searching for the father who dressed her
for a wedding
she has chosen her own path
made her vows, and grown lean
standing on one leg after another
bent to a will

the wind reveals her pride

magnifies the bones she stands on
the egret looks to the sun to light her spirit
covered by plumes of pretences
she wills the wind to lift her feathers
air, grains, smells and all

i am a hump of sandcastle
filled with unspeakable dreams
through the window of her eyes
i see the sun hiding, brooding
startled by the darkness that lives there

here in badagry, egrets walk over graves
of poems, filled with empty metaphors
paths lead over exposed roots
across paths bleached as skeletons
and the wind mutters incantations
willing me: rise from the dead

here, where my river bends
i am lost in sand, ankle deep in dung

take me there where my river ends
and night begins to woo his bride,
take me there where waves laugh
mocking our silence
rising to slap her swollen breasts
against our shore

the wind bids:
                suckle and write the poem of your life
                fill your bucket with better than sand

empty, i cross myself, thinking
life is not religious
a poem is not a river
there is more sand in the world
than water

by a dump

i
how terribly you smell my country
a fall collection of
empty bottles
unfinished meals
and broken seats

heap of discarded dreams

ii
hungry mongrels scavenge
find drumsticks
shells and
bones

they growl over
the rotten meal
of our hopes

iii
sycophantic flies
buzz familiar lies
spindle hands clasped
in grace
over our spoils

praise singers of decay
familiar spirits you claim your own

iv
urchins dressed in torn
hymn books
poke through your putrid
promises
priests of impoverished prayers
seeking bone, they find

dismembered dreams
and wasted poems

remnants of bitter lives

v
cloud of flies rises
salutes the plangent poet
of our pungent pile
buzzes a song, happy

to celebrate our sores
happy to dance over our spoils

vi
and our spoils are many, my country
all over this dump
mouth open
teeth diseased
bare to the gum

you perfume the air
with the flesh
of dying days

vii
i see you wear once more
that petty coat of waste
i have come to know

i see flies rise and hear
their lament of praise

our mongrels chew our bone
lick our marrow
and discard what is left

we have become refuse refused

even by dogs

i swallow your putrid pill
and become one with waste

viii
your children cover their sores
food too for flies
with tattered bits of our flag
our green and off white
as they poke, search
and find only fragments
of decaying dreams

rotting, we rot with you
dying, we die with you
my country

voyages
barcelona

when the laughter goes
and the spirits leave our eyes
it is the tale of our common love
wreathed by humps of hills
and of the sun going to sleep
covered in blazing duvet of glory
which remains

remembering nsukka

to uzo anucha

when the laughter goes
and the spirits leave our eyes
it is the tale of our common love
wreathed by humps of hills
and of the sun going to sleep
covered in blazing duvet of glory
which remains

the voice that speaks is unspeaking
like the soul
kneeling before st teresa's grotto
calmed by the years and many mile
        stones
and a simple wish
never to forget

how the heart holds like a river
a school of memories

here, where flowers turn their collars up
and streams stretch languid arms
around rocks for a hug
i found a heart filled with herbs
filled as the soil with roots

there, by the puddle by slessor
        it leads to a deeper earth
        being kinder than the cloud
        it holds on to memory
i saw our eyes look back with dreams
weightier than a book

there, by the lonely brook of onu iyi
the priestess wore feathers round her slim waist
feet covered with nzu and virgin fronds

she laughed, she cried
          she sang, she danced
drunk on the wine of enugu ezike
she ate white fowl with ose nsukka
and pulled out a feather for my head

many harmattans later
i still wear her spell like a crown

you have given me a kolanut bowl
therein lie our finest lobes
all our history, all our roads
all my yearnings

the chief priest cautions, bite slowly
they are bitter, they are
          bitter
for life is wrung out of onugbu

here in sage
waist deep in benin's flash flood of fears
i find teeth for the suya you offer
your bits and floral adventures
it is maple syrup creamed cookies
it is foreign and ancient and native
and breathing

just like memory

grey

flying over the atlantic
one cannot simply fathom
the limitlessness of god
his depth and expanse

i am grey and limited
like an amputated arm

clouds stroll down main street
like tourists, naive and burdened
hanging on nothing but
their immense aloofness

a rainbow appears like ribbon
arched with fire and temptation
colours flow down, fade into grey
my earth is far away
through the veil of rain
nonchalant and brilliantly dour
covered only by what is dreamed

i too am without soil
without substance
without even simple drops of dew

fingers of rain calligraph a sign
on my window pane
i can see the other side
see randy rain fall from grace
into mortal sin
pulled down by the force
of familiar notions

i flow away, into eternity
become one with the sea
perplexed drop that falls away

mingles with the clouds
and vaporises like thought

i fear when the next rain falls
i too will fall with it
mingle with other floating spirits
yet you will not tell me
from bodies of falling water
such is the immensity of things

london aisles

i.   walking

been walking all my life

looking for destinations
i find only detours
many streets lead away from picadilly circus
make life a maze of jokes
and unfinished starts

life here they say has no bumps
i manage to find them
it is my special gift
i step into nonevident potholes
they swallow my dreams

i bury my head
to find lasting peace
as realism bites
with molars of winter

who am i, i often ask
what binds me to this ground
as i circle trafalgar square
too many tourists, voyeurs
pellets of plastic smiles
cameras melt frozen faces
tongues i cannot master

i have a life i cannot own

why do these pigeons laugh
why are their feathers full of anecdotes
white and grey
feet quick to the touch

why are these lions black
why are their teeth blunt
they laugh with stolid faces
feed on crumbs of moods
pride set in stone

why is the wind crying
bitter
calling my name
above this whisper

the london cold drives
righthanded
towards me
drives me off the edge
into the muttering thames

i swim inside myself
feeling
groping
floundering like a wave

i wipe away tears

ii.   flickering

i can't wrap my fingers
around this shadow

into droplets of grief
i stroke the cloud

is it my soul i see
flickering in the distance

is it my voice i hear
trailing an ebbing light

it is so far away
and i am lost

iii.   stars

it is all
dark

far away

i flicker
into
bits
of
essence

iv.   homeland

the soul yawns
tired
reveals a cave,
dark and empty

some days too
are dark

inside
rats, bats
and stalactites,
snakes,
live
along tribal lines
each with his own
tongue
each with his own
devil's mark

further down
inside the heart
of ogbunike,
my homeland,
there lives too
a pond of collected
grief

and a hunchback
of aso-tired rocks
dragging everything
down

holding everyone
down

v.   canvas

i am
a blank canvas

doing nothing
i stare
into thin
air

vacant

you are a
palette
of temptations

vi.   melody

slowly
you open to me
budding flower
filled with nectar

bee, i buzz
around those petals
pouch swollen
filled with melody

and sting

vii.   diamond

i am a rough
cut
diamond

you fill me
with light,
sharp facets

and many inter
          sections

viii.   beauty

the beauty
of the world
like your skin
makes love
to my eyes

joyous
i grow bold
like blossoms

ix   dream

love engulfs me like duvet
even in this cold
it must be your animal hug
and the fire in your breast

i snuggle closer
smell your native fragrance
and feel your breath of grapes
you are a vineyard of tenderness
cellar of pressed passions

the heat of your body
microwaves my dreams
the slow heat and spices
and my mouth waters
filled with desire

you are more real
than this voice i hear
through the dark of sleep
you hum our songs
holding me close, whispering
         how real memories become
         in the cold

you are more warm
than this brutal night
more real than
this kate middleton

barcelona blues

i.   anthills

we stand as anthills
each with his own tales,
a million termites of ideas
teem within, hidden away
from prying eyes, as we
speak, unveiling little

some work their way
to the surface: a smile, raised
brows, the sun and a shoot,
a train of words carefully chosen
run one after another
on a stiff set track of prejudices

and a world beneath light
is revealed

vivian jamal speaks with song
mouth filled with grapes of humour
or perhaps it is my ears
choosing what to hear from one
so lovely, like petals of lilies
choosing their sweet drops of rain

effiong knows my tongue, follows
my voice, a trail of fireflies,
many stairways down our cave
he sees me, iphone in hand,
covered in mud, moulding
my usual blocks of poems
for those who will rise to the top
and find light

marta crouches away from all, queen ant

communing with spirits, her voice
lost in the hum; xandy clutches
a book of stories, some pages frayed
edited of metaphor and hope;
aniya! aniya!, your smile fills the room
with conversations

everyone with his own tales, alone
even in this tiled crowd

so we stand alone, anthills
working to the surface, bits
of mud seeking water, teacups
of warm ideas in hand, sipping
our dreams by the depressed hills
of barcelona

seeking different paths out of our tunnels

ii.   without you

without you
my morning is grey
misted over with memories
of faded smiles

without you
my windows, rattled by
the wind and ohs! moan
like a starved mongrel,
the chill finds its stubborn way in
nibbles at my toes

without you
barcelona is a city in refuge
like homeless nadia, hiding
her forlorn heart
inside the woolen sweater
of this grey morning

iii.   sometimes the sun

sometimes
the sun finds me crouching
under duvets, too
afraid to share my sole
with the cold floor, afraid
to share my day with
a cold world

too cold inside for life
outside

you are too far away
like the moon, the light
of memory does not warm me
dark spots live under the foliage
of loneliness
here in barcelona

iv.   you are more than the sun

you are more than the sun
when you smile, and
i cannot look at you
and not be blinded, owl
before a sudden explosion
of headlights

alas you are too far away
like the sun
and the spectre of your smile
just the spectre, bathes me
like warm water from a fiddled faucet

i cannot think of your smile
and not become warm

to share barcelona with you
i reinvent you thus, ipad in hand
take you in small pages, in
small glances behind my oakley,
to see you and not go blind,
to feel you and not be scalded, not
go mad from sudden pleasures

to share my day with you
i hide inside myself
browsing our moments in small
pictures, and grow warm
become wanton with words

i cannot think of you
and not be warmed
you are more than the sun
when you smile

v.   birds are overrated

birds simply are overrated
and so are all these signs
of awakening: light, sounds
and people shaking off sleep
losing the darkness that binds us
as prisoners to our backside

lustily birds sing, flowers too
and cars eating through pedralbes
for what? about what? why?
freedom? joy? light?
or hunger stirring with life
in the belly of this rising city?

their eyes hold all the light
of day, any way
all the colours, all vision
and sensation, selfish that way

birds sing for themselves
as do flowers in the garden of statues
their words bear nothing
of my loneliness

being selfish in their awakening

vi.   i cannot be free of you, barcelona

i cannot be free of you, barcelona
even now, as i draw the thick curtains of
victoria suites
to keep your stubborn summer lights away
and settle into the warm arms of nigeria

your laughter by the beaches of old barcelona,
sharing jokes with the mediterranean, as gently
it slapped your thighs, still rings in my ears
futilely stuffed with monologues of iese;
old barcelona where silence is dearer
than flesh and haunting aromas of dying

smiles of pedralbes shine brightly still
with your sun, along your boulevards, unending
as the grand temple of sagrada familia, gathering
your blocks and sweat to build a monument
to the gods; the magnificent montjuïc still holds
the footprints of your forbears; listen gently
and hear their mantra in the wind, in
the majestic font magica whose waters rise above
our heads, to nourish and not to drown

they all return as i close my eyes, all of you
barcelona; plaça de catalunya, the long walk
down the rambla, where shoulders brush
their loneliness against the bruised canvas
of old walls; spices of mercat de la boqueria
hold the nostrils hostage and float on the
ceiling as apparitions of hunger

you are everywhere, as i walk through your
arc de triomf: visitor, student, disciple,
conqueror;

63

i stand before torre agbar and see
how little man is, and grand the thoughts of his mind,
at monument a colom, memorial of madness to columbus
i see how far a dream can travel, many brutal
frontiers we tame when we put one foot after another

and i walk again towards you, arms held wide
seeking embrace, seeking communion, seeking repose

nothing can keep you away, barcelona: guardian,
mother, spirit;
you run your marathons in my veins, paint
in my heart the art of picasso; your laughter rings through
and breaks the tarpaulin tough of these curtains
as your lights, your lights barcelona, shine brightly
through eyes that cannot remain shut for the night

nothing can keep you away
when the heart is filled with pleasure and madness
and love for you, my barcelona

vii.   my eyes run over your length

my eyes, deepened by time and distance,
run over your length, my barcelona
woman with arrogant nipples
upon crested hills

i part your trees as limbs
to spy where the sun hides
with its boundless light and gifts
you are lush with petals of
purpled preening, endowed
with spice and fragrance

i watch you come to me, sashaying
as sara, filled with curious tongues
and delight; your beauty is in your
strangeness, exotic bellies of your
flamenco belles, your resolute statues

and i come to you, camera in my head
the one from which all the words
and images come, snapping and
writing, and loving like this

barcelona, your hands fold me into you   .
warm and soft as fresh loaves
you are the woman in whom my poetry
takes root, and springs to life
your milk nourishes it, endows
it with an immortal soul

to leave you is to exorcise myself
to rid myself of spirit and madness
to leave you, my barcelona, is
to take my lips off your nipples
and starve on the cold tormenting sidewalks
of london; homeless, without love

viii. your statues

your statues stand cold
and unfeeling
they are your patron saints
they took the whip for you
and emptied into you
their spirit and gospel

in you their blood flows too
in you they emptied every blood
so they stand now, lifeless, in a place
for you, naked but for a few petals
for your boulevards that teem
with the blood and sweat of a people

like now, barcelona
a hundred feet pound your pavements
running, everyone runs in this city
as the sun, reluctant and kind
lowers itself to bed behind your hills

everyone runs around your statues
before your statues, because of
your statues, your guardians, your
spirits; not teasing, but
worshipful

because your statues have taken all your whip
and made of you a perpetual resurrection

ix.   clouds look the same

clouds look the same from here
as i leave london, lot's wife
farstretching, fluffy, white
and filled with your waters
but my heart tells me my eyes lie
nothing is like you, my barcelona

nothing was like you, my love
woman with the provocative eye
when, briefly, in my arms you lay
and i kissed your flowers of soft lips, felt
through my veins
your warm juice flow to my heart
where no stronger walls hold in their lodgings
love for a woman

streets of london wear the same clothes
the trees, the flowers, jackets of tiled houses
and arteries of roads cleansed of cholesterol
but no blood flows like yours
the trees, the flowers, the arteries
no wind, baptised by the mediterranean
carries a deeper fragrance; no sun

has warmed me, barcelona, as yours
on the plastic plains of europe

you are barcelona, you are
nothing like the clouds i see from here
empty of life and water, just empty
like fluffy balls of cotton

you are barcelona, you are
my barcelona
you are nothing
like these cold clouds that come and go

manhattan

i return to you with sadness
this is not the affair we proclaimed
you with your lights of august
soft fur of evening and flames
when you wrapped me in warmth and whisper
and i, with my hungry poems
and african eyes of innocence

you brewed fear
into a warm mug of welcome
many seasons ago
and threw bouquets of bleeding hearts
into the hudson for me

how our days become watered down
our evenings filled with sighs of regret
and everywhere melancholy emerges
from mists of stubbed days

are you this body of wind
heaving from silences
shredded by the sharp edge of panes
            and broken lives
into these bitter b i t s of lamentations?

are you these red lips
cheap fragrance and
flaming eyes
this diseased hand asking
            can you spare a quarter?

what embrace comes this empty?
what smile strips our days of flowers
our nights of stars?

our days are so possessed

of sophistry and small talk
of fire and bonfires
of flesh and soul

our nights are
an unchained motion and stillness
pleasure and pain
cries and these still silences

manhattan, manhattan
with you my nights become a lament
                ancient and pyramidal
and i see your vagrant spirit
haggle its way through the night

i see your lights flicker from green
to yellow and become red, blood red
as you drift, with slow death
from the stub of evening
into darkness

reborn

for siobhan and her harp

i sit with you and i am lost
in a world of sounds and magic
fly away with hummingbirds
in whose wings, as your fragile fingers
are a thousand melodies
and the softness of dream

my soul curls round those fingers
feline of phantom fevers
as you date my life with mystery
                and music
i resonate in the silences
between stanzas
drown in the calm of your eyes

my spirit nests in those eyes
there it takes wings
reborn as eagle
becomes this phoenix that dies
in the ashes of my fears
and resurrects, soars with joy
searches out a familiar shore
in the tropics of my mind

i grow into nothing
in that horizon you conjure
lost like smoke

                it is what we share
                this sorcery and wild sunsets
                this dancing over river thames

a journey of many miles comes to this
this lifting and drowning
this becoming and loss

the beauty of your eyes
lures me from the edge
and i smile
find my usual solitary dusk

and dawn

it is for this moment i become reborn
pilgrim
poet
psalmist

returning home
for omar

my first view of you
is of our waters
peeping through dark clouds
some dark dawn

they say a dark cloud is an omen
its quiver full of arrows
and water is worse
when one cannot swim

we have floundered through the years
you and i who neither swim nor
sow, who till a farm in the air, who

watch from our perch on the rock
waters overflow farmlands
drown rivers, roads, even
bridges, drown roots, drown
that last fading harvest

we flounder still, you and i
seeking footholds we grab at
drifting clouds, fall off our
limited sky and sink

sink, all of us, sink with
every dark cloud, every
drone of fear, every click
of a seatbelt that holds us
down, immobilised, not moving
forward, not moving at all

we go down, all of us
with the stubborn dream that
some day
we would land on solid ground

garlands

ebele

under this mango tree
you are ripe and edible
and everywhere
purring and caressing and whispering
that you love me

ebele

i distil you with lines of my poem
light of dew
watch you ornament dawn with your petals
fresh and filled with colours
and it becomes something intoxicating
becomes the spirit grapes sacrificed
to the wine

you are the secret the wind shares
with the flute
pulsing
melodious and
of the finest stem

i see the paintings your skin becomes
in the light of evening
they enflame your hills, your valleys
infuse your offerings with the deepest sorcery

your colours are delicious like mangoes
contours coy as chocolate
and i bite into you, holding
you melt
you flow
submit to the tongue
transcend flesh, pleasure
and imaginings

you are formed of the finest fibre
woven into the loveliest silk
you are the gentlest breeze, my love
and you make the air rise, gather feet,
run across the plains like a lover

> my heart swells like sail
> filled with the most talismanic fever

my lips tremble as pine with elegant lines
you become mystical
written into epic passages

you are the joy my heart wears like fragrance
my finest verse
and i perfume you with poems
anoint you with their oil
drape you with pearls, petals
and the most delicate silk

springtime

i   you come as flute

you come as flute that fills the air
with warm longings
and around me
it is as though birds sing
the warm dawn of your eyes

roses bloom too, o how they bloom
in the springtime of your smile
and i am lost
vagrant leaf clawing in the warm air
at nonexistent footholds
butterfly seeking nectar
and rare pollens

        bright light of sunset
        you hold darkness at bay

you come clothed with fire
        and blood
and flow like lava
consuming in your path all my gestating doubts
all my lack of sound and song
and i singe as rocks of those weeping hills
        untameable vapours of delight
sing when you flow over my soul this way

ii   i gather my day in a garden

i gather my day in a garden of flowers
and in your eyes of light
they bloom as in springtime
bloom as though you gather to your heart
bouquets to decorate these longings

whiff of jasmine and queen of night
you pass and fragrances follow
like a faithful pooch
and, about the soft flowers of your smile,
the butterflies of my heart flutter

        ah therefrom i am perfumed and thus
        become
           my poems powdered by those fragile wings
           shedding beauty with each beat

you smile as begonia that blooms
your luscious lips tender as canna
when from your eyes the softness of stars drop
as dew, drop as rain
and my heart becomes the warm day
that flings the rainbow, bowed by beauty
across a happy sky

you bloom with verdure of spring
with petals of pleasure and
butterflies of buttered buntings
and the soft soil of my heart is manured
yields to this budding of song:

        beauty like bouquets
        beauty like butterflies
        beauty beyond sunsets
        beauty
        beyond beauty

made this way

you collect gems of joy in your eyes
white light of history
          and expedition
pupils deep as space, intimate as a hug
and over your cherub face
i paint my past

over your warm luscious body
fumbling, i find myself
spreading a linen of fresh habits

you are made this way
box of chocolates and strawberries
brooch i wear over my heart as totem
          and promise
you are minted as rare coin
and here i melt you, naïve as candy
on the tongue of the poem

          you are made this way
          without guile, without guile
          you are filled with love as grapes
          with juice of intimate pleasure

the moon, naked but for a necklace
of stars, smiles because you smile
slowly, for you, she grows full bosomed
ah, you are beautiful, little flower
sudden pond of light, haloed hills
of jos

you are this new legume
sprouting, fragile
breath of earth
          ripe and tender smells

you are this fine linen of joy
this melting as butter of my heart
and on your lucent skin of light
without fear
without fear
my dawn collects
its goose bumps
of dew

ambience

sitting under a mango tree
after tennis at grand hotel
watching the thrifty niger
break out in little pimples
the breeze purrs and caresses like a lover
and leaves fall and the exposed white sand
gleams with coyness

children frolic in the water
laughing with the teeth of egrets
they echo your spirit when you are happy
capture in their eyes your soul

and my easter is content
because sweat falls to the caressing breeze
waters chuckle as they hug the reeds
and the reeds, teary eyed, swooning
bow their necks for a kiss

leaves whisper as though
we are sharing secrets
as the shrubs eavesdrop, bending closer
ears of tender petals

easter is beautiful because you are here
            and everywhere
and sadness crouches like a crab
on the other shore
walking sideways
eating sand

under this mango tree
you are ripe and edible
            and everywhere
purring and caressing and whispering
that you love me

flames

i look at you
my eyes redden like flame
with desire

i think of you
my heart bursts into flames
with anthems of praise

i see you
dressed like cherry blossoms
in the flaming evening
i melt into a lava
of liquefied longing

i utter your name
simple as ★ ★ ★
and persistent as fire
i am scalded
words leap out like a tongue
of a thousand flames

i will take your lips

i will take your lips
and turn them into grapes
soft, succulent and sweet
hold them tenderly
squeeze
and taste the fresh juice that flows
surely

i will take your eyes
full of life and gently bright
with light on dew,
turn them into jewels
watch them light up my universe
as stars

your skin is soft butter and
brilliant sheen of light
and i make it into this velvet
        of valentine verses
i watch the rivers of warm blood
        turn all golden
and blue bells bloom all over you

your voice for me becomes
this symphony of birds
serenading the beauty of dawn
and the dawn of beauty
and i mould it into melody
lovely, just as you are

worship

it is the catechism of your eyes
that drew me first to worship
deep and unfathomable
they were the waters of the sea
where i, as aladuras, camp out
night and day
to conjure pleasures only the faithful
can see

and there are many, those pleasures
standing where passion and origins
embrace with laughter
the pleasure of coming home to shore
of lifting into the air, clapping as waves
running with joy into your arms as a child
teeth white as sea sand
rooted to grains of delicious days

you coil around the ankle of my mind
mewing with pleasure
warm as embrace
soft as tenderness

your eyes too are soft as flesh
soft as hymns of meditation
you are eternal as the sky
unending as waters of the sea
as petitions that call calm waters
to rise as wanton wave and wish

in you all the riches of pleasure live
in me, all the diverse and faithful tongues

lost

i am not what i used to be
i am lost in a world i do not own

every space belongs to you
every form
every fibre
every air

every tree bears your ripe fruits
every road your infinite promise
every sound
every heartbeat
you inhabit them all

i am not what i used to be
i am what you have made of me

lost in a world you own

my heart begins to go

my heart begins to go again
on its familiar dash
racing, i am sure
to the trophy of your smile, and
those eyes gleaming with medals of gold

i pant, unmanned by my lack of fitness
and composure
i am no olympian you see
so sometimes i simply sit quietly
measuring my faith
against the bulging biceps of uncommon desires

i measure myself against familiar dreams
once more i come up short
come up against the wildly shrieking words
of open plains
plain as i am plain
plain against the specific light
the truly specific light of your smile

you smile and your eyes smile
your pores smile
your hair of dark nights twinkle
with many stars
and i, without steroids,
with too much hope perhaps
measure myself against uncertain leaps
of faith

distance adds a poignant edge

distance adds a poignant edge to our longings
and words that bridge the clouds
are heavy with forbidden promises
stoked into a fine flame of desire

you are made this way
sorceress of unformed shadowy words of desire
your eyes an unending well of mysteries
lips full and soft like ripe cherries
        fecund and fair

        you are made this way
        without space
        without sibilance
        filled with distance and awe

distance sharpens to a flint our longings
and the words, comfortless, bring to a quiver
the void where only a moment ago
you bronzed my day
like a finely crafted artefact

do i love you then
as a fine piece of old longing?
do i hug your soft contours
as this pillow
enrobing memories?

do i love you as the warm light of dawn
when dew melts on leaves
and, unseen, drifts into the air with desire
unmasking the veins
unmasking my blood
and my heart beats a path of rivers to you

at night, at night

when substance melts into shadow
and the shadow, as i
whispers without comfort
i shape you into a dream
and float away like a broken plume
on a quivering of desires

but day comes
and your absence digs into the rib
of everything
a fine, sharpened edge

achile

a child makes up the world
a drop of water the universe
it is in your eyes of light
deep and ancient as the soul

your eyes of infinite dream
maps the world
reveals molecules of earth
your enigma
pods of truth
the pristine pleasures of being

you smile as the sun that awakes
each smile a ray of pleasure
each pleasure a drop of light
each smile reveals you, achile
at once translucent and far off

you enter my empty dark places, my
forsaken warehouse
like an eye of light
and reveal each grain of dust
particles of mysteries we inhale
without knowing, clueless
in our rank lack of purpose

perhaps you are endless
perhaps you are a journey
a single step leads into a forest of mysteries
perhaps you multiply pleasure
and pain
evoke song and dust
write them into a melody

you shape my heart into a pen
and fill it with blood and ink

each squeeze reveals a drop
each drop lengthens into a poem
becomes this poem that becomes you
a verse,
the universe

you are a simple name
etched like a star in the dark
and it becomes the firmament
endless like a journey
endless like life

a child makes up the world
drop of water the universe
·it is in your eyes of light
deep and ancient as the soul

how i want to hold you

how i want to hold you
as i hold this pen
            tenderly
worshipfully as crucifix
you who are slender as exclamation
upright as poplar
inhabited by all the wonders of desire

            forgive these unlearned hands
            which bruise your tender ribs in a coarse hug
            and stoke thus out of your hearth
            all the words contained as fire in the belly of coals

from you all the words of wonder flow
all the words of desire
all the words of despair
the current of love and the torrent of hurt
rainbow bent at the edge by the wet sorrow of grey things
the trees of jos bent low under the lowing of the plains

you flow like currents of warm air
and murmur like the waters
you who are every word
every sign, every whisper
every sigh
you drift through leaves and alight upon my waters
vivid with memory
fluid, fragrant and fragile

you who are sharp like a nib
fluid like a nib
fragile like a nib
you who are friend and foe
song and scent
water and spirit

from you all the words of wonder flow

all the letters of the poem
and you call out from my simple soul
all the wonders, dark and liquid
spreading out on leaves of innocence thus
with sudden exclamations

      how i want to hold you
          tenderly
                worshipfully
          wistfully
      inhabited by all the wonders of the word

chi oma

your eyes tell many stories
of courage and strength
murmurs and groans that give african nights
their spell and music
and i listen to all of them
listen to you tell the beating of your heart

grandmother told them beautifully too
in the light of the full moon
that sauntered down our hill, in the light
that sprinkled a thousand stars upon my rivers
in the light of your smile, in the light
of your lonesome eyes

she told of you, of those eyes
filled with longing as breeze,
fingers soft and nimble
tickling young fronds to quiver and fret
being virginal like me

thus i build my own tales, write
with my blood and sperm poems of you
and here i begin to build in the air
castles of words, uninhabitable castles
form fantastic febrile fables:

of you smiling again with those eyes
of you passing by, tickling, tickling
of you wrapped in the white sheet of a full moon
lounging at every corner of our courtyard
with your many tales

of you cooing like the waters, filling
my parched pen with a poem, saying:
        'you have a way with words'
and as an afterthought:

'you have such gentle eyes
it must be the poetry'

this you say is your first poem
this i say is testament and communion:
man with beauty, man with chi oma
chi di nma
       chi di ebube
man with the immeasurable memorable memorials
of life

sounds tell me the world out there lives

it began with a taste of your lips
and white eyes of palm wine
and i am drunken
filled with wine of love for your company

your words of grapes, distilled and
bottled in the cellar of my heart
these many years
burst loose
mimic merriment in their explosion
balls of seduction for my parched palate

i faint to think how many drops of regret
have coloured my tongue grey
how many grains of dust
i have acquired like taste, worn like loincloth
cobwebs dancing without rhythm
swinging in senseless stupor, just swinging
in the cold and bitter and intoxicating emptiness
of memory

how many times i have climbed steps of reason
finding ghosts, prisms
and too many reasons just to climb
you are gone like time, never to return
only tolling moments
only pain falling over itself like steps
in a fused flight of years

a bar of light peeps through the crack
beneath the door
which barricades me from rihanna, other lips
of grapes and mint
and the world out there

sounds tell me the world out there lives

birds, moments and silences
i hear my loss uncoil into sighs
see my breath become smoke
in this pale pall of pain

hmmm becomes an epic
and from the gourd of memory
tall, broad hipped like you
        and fragile
i sip thoughts of you
and lapse into my usual stupor
and regret

i want to be loved simply

i want to be loved
simply
as butterflies flowers
they gather to their wings
colours to clothe our garden

i want to be loved
as bees nectar
abuzz with joy
and sweethearted
building in its belly
honey to heal our days

i want to be loved
as pines the wind
guilelessly
upright without airs
strumming symphonies
with fine fingers

i want to be loved
as sun earth
keenly, greening life
so affectionate it fragments into
stars
lace of sequined diamonds
for your dark body

i want to be loved
faithfully
as queen of the night
that breathes into our darkness
endowed
with your fragrances

i want to be loved simply

plunder

i will take these moments with you
without fear
without remorse
this plunder
digging as they do for diamonds
into your earth

this is our rite of thunder
for it rains in our hearts a flood of misery
and our groans, like these rumbles
bemoan the darkness that covers us

pray, what more can it be?
with what fear can the chicken weep?
what more suffering
can draw blood from our eyes?

we have sold our hearts
for privations of pleasure
bound only to this release
when we must stand,
bereft of tenderness.
and walk away

how can you know

how can you know my heart
when it beats too slowly for you

your feet, cockroach quick
fly across the dance hall
and i cannot keep pace
the music muscles its way
finds a heap of broken hearts
murmuring its way to the grave
        yard

i cannot master the fluidity of ice
its tongue is razor sharp
and in a pool of its own blood
slowly it dies
it is my love, strangely suicidal
lacking the will to remain strong

how can you know my heart
when it lies drained
impaled at your cross
        roads
too slow to keep pace

tepid

slowly we drift apart
fingers grow numb
recoil like touchanddie
our voices thin, lose their nerve
lose their way like a desert,
we can no longer hear each other
hear the plaintive pleas
of hearts in love

all we do now is stutter
through battered feelings

our song comes to the last note
we slow down, feet unsure
lacking rhythm
        like driftwood
lacking spark
        only thunder
lacking the quickening
which brings a face to smile
flowers to a plant
our feelings to their old shine

our fire goes out, only cinders
and my fever breaks
it is the quinine in your
tongue, the flood in your eyes
carrying a sack of bitterness

our path stops at the edge of a clearing
it is a forest, deep and terrifying
teeming with wild plants, broken
twigs and ancestral spirits
dressed in nothing but raffia
and our masks

soon it grows dark

our love a shape in the distance
your face grows dark too, loses its lines
becomes one with the shadows
becomes this wall into which, naked
i walk

slowly we grow tepid
become this forsaken cup of coffee
black
and bitter
and without warmth

jos this morning

i run my words as loving fingers
all over you
your skin of olives and electricity
whisper them quietly certain valentine evenings
as the sun whispers to the skin
certain jos mornings

and you glow as oil
smooth and transparent as your heart
of crystals

i love you as birds the quickening dawn
the warm fingers of the sun
run through their feathers
and raise a choir in their breasts

i love you with hunger and song
with my poem and my pain
i love you as the hills that weep
at height of noon
thrilled, just thrilled
to feel warm light in their eyes

jos unfolds this morning
as your skin to my caresses
as you salvage my heart from
the cold compress of a bitter night

you chase it away, you chase
the cold away, my love
this cold compress of silence
as your warmth engulfs my city
and my soul
this day

as i love you

nobody will love you as i love you
adorned with rivers and light
you are wide as the earth
filled with riches and mud
and i walk barefoot
feeling your blood seep through
feel you tremble and groan

in the skies i too quiver with fevers
ready to drench you with my love
lo a flash tears through the night
and i quicken with rain
become intense as waterfalls
i bath you, make you new
pour out your native smell upon the earth

our fire reveals your face
as i embrace you, holding as a child
you open your lips as petals
open your heart as a book to me
your arms hold me as religion, firm
with promise and gospel
and i worship you, sing of you
as the flute that worships ijele

you are all the poems of joy
all the plants of spring, breaking forth
with softness and the finest colours
you are, my love, the leaves of ivy
holding my wall by the waist like a lover
your eyes two streams of desire
flowing down the bemused hills of jos

nobody will love you as i love you
as the waters that bear their riches
contained within the bed of a river
flowing without cease

my poems will cover you

i will cover you with all the garments of love
silk, satin and laces
adorn your bougainvillea with beads
and i will crown you with gele so grand
you hold the sun in your hair

i will dress you
in all the fine fabrics of love
covered with my kisses, my life
my melancholia
i will rub all over you my exuberance and oil
and i shade your eyes so the fire burns
gently

this way will i love you
with flowers, phrases and fragrances
with emeralds, pearls
and all the tender fires of earth
on your slender fingers, your dark neck
and from the branch of your ears
dangle fragile fruits of glittering gems

they are cool, my love
yet with you they become fiery
imbued with passion and light
made special by the brilliant sunset
that does not set in your eyes

you are full and fulfilled
your contours make my garments warm
              and articulate
as plants and grasses cover earth's nakedness
leaves and flowers the phallic frigidity of plants
my rivers weep over your lounging beauty
my woman, my earth

my poems will cover you

make you more than human
more than this woman who loses herself
naked
shorn of all self
to my tender, probing hands

pool

sitting
by the pool of your smile
i see light rise in our eyes
reveal all prisms of joy
and i hear you breathe
hear love whisper as the breeze
that nuzzles the pines into tenderness

you ripple as the waters
grow as waves into tempest
you grow too into something delicate
        and intimate
into something to behold and to bite
you are berries and all the fruits of endearment
your lips full, pursed
for the kiss that seals our treachery

i pick your smile and pop into my mouth
you burst into many stories
you are this pomegranate, this tangerine
you are sweet and tangy
multilayered like a river
with drops of translucent joy

the glass bowl of your eyes
reveals many idioms and tongues of fire
you are full of pleasure
full of sweet turns of phrase, piquant
and juicy

away from you

away from you, you are not away from me
everywhere i take you with me
not as air i cannot shake off
but, obi'm, in the beating
and the blood

you are in every thing, you are everything
you are as much everywhere as you are
within my heart
most certainly here, you are here
under the dimpled dusk of ibom resort
watching the golf balls, white and dimpled too
sail through the air to find rest
in that inner place of the heart

    you make heavy my breath
        with longing
    as flowers waltz to fluted songs, swoon
    to the subtle sound of my poems

far off we lounge as the green lawns,
lying side by side as the crouching hills
rolling on the lush green duvet
as often we do

away from you, lost in the sublime mist
lost in the rolling memories, head in the
clouds that visit at dawn with rays of your smile
everything becomes you,
becomes the memories we build
with architectural elegance, with love

away from you, you are not away from me
you are in everything, you are everything
you are, obi'm, the beating of my heart
the blood and the air

my morning begins with you

my morning begins with many sounds
birds, cars, voices
trees
life outside the window of my heart
but it is of you breathing softly
beside me
i hear most eloquently

we journey through seasons and places
feel the moments come to us as milestones
and night brush off its dark apparel stars
we feel the rain fall with silence and rage
cleaved to each other as a leaf to a branch

we are built for this:
silence and thunder, my love
alone like this, away from all the world
and its wearying worries
inhaling life and our redolent madness

inhaling only
starved

your sounds suffuse my awakening
and drown mine, though silent,
roaring like waterfalls within
they say it is dread
they say it is the end of innocence
and my day

but you are my morning too
and i hear nothing else
no birds, no cars, no voices
just you breathing
just you, warm naked flesh
and silence

your touch

your touch is all i crave now
your fire and lightning
that set me alight, burn
when you are far away
like now

when you are here
the current surges
my skin burns without scalding
and my heart quickens,
crackling

i rise and smile,
satiated

spirits and fire

slowly i sip from the goblet of your lips
you are more cognac than juice
filled with spirits and fire
warm, you search out my heart
and there set fire

i burn
my lips burn for a taste of your lips
my flesh burns with fever, laid out as sacrifice
over your unconquerable shrine, over
your body of palms, neck of poplar
over your rolling plains teeming
with whispering pines

my heart burns, laid out on a grille
sauteed and tenderised
my heart burns, drains blood from my lips of coals
empties my heart of fear
and i hunger for you, grow grave
like a ravine

on my parched lips your spirits alight
like a bird on a branch that is
the branch of my soul
and i feel you cast your spell
downwards
your flames and tempest
feel you fill me with your love
more fiery than cognac

you are a cauldron, you are a lake
and your eyes hold on their surface
your depth and soul

among your bushes

i will weave on your soft skin
a lingerie with my kisses
run a thread of pleasures
to your intimate places
and on the wet path by the thicket
stoke a fire that will burn,
without burning,
so bright it frames your face in my hands
and casts shadows into the night

my hands will journey
over your special places
your altars, totems
and warm spring
to visit and savour;
your hairs will stand at attention
saluting the fingers that worship your body

among your bushes, in your rich foliage
and over the smooth trunk of your limbs
i go as your hunter, finger on trigger
searching for bushmeat, pussy
cats and antelopes with a crown
of decorated gifts

you will feel the earth move
my wheels slow and deliberate as a train of
tenderness and heart's twister,
my tracks mark your savannah
leave your leaves aquiver with eagerness

on your baobab, in your undergrowth
across your hidden paths and ponds
are many nests of pleasure, fruits
and fountains of life

i jaunt down the pathway of your body

i jaunt down the pathway of your body
it is early dawn
and dew is young again
on your low lying grasses

the shadow of your lashes lengthens over me
i crouch in the cool calm
counting leaves that flutter
when you look at me this way

the sun still hides in the grey clouds of your eyes
it is early dawn
dark as you are dark
heavy with multiplying mysteries
and i pick my way through the crack of your smile
the earlydawn chill of unfinished words

light fingers of wind rustle the flora
lifting their skirt when you walk by

at dusk
the sun pauses over a lonely cloud
to stare, running a singleminded eye
over your winsome length, over
your bouquet of dazzling flowers
and in the dying light
the sun strains to come back to life

it is halflight
and i jaunt down the pathway of your body
darkened by desire, straining to rise to life
but the mysteries multiply, as stars
multiply as dunes into a gathering of loose sand
when your breath blows over my length

star

it is because you twinkle thus
you see me dancing on clouds

you flow into me with your light
        and softness
and lifted and light
        headed
my feet cannot keep still

i cannot remain grounded
i dance with your star

joy

i float on joy
when i am with you
my heart is a spring
of fresh waters, flowing
freely

in your river
i find many treasures

your currents call me
i am your driftwood
i swim wherever you go
floating on nothing
but love

ache

shrubs possess me
possess this hibiscus i call a head
and there you are
red, soft and many sided
brilliantly coloured flower
your pollens, pointing, poke the sun

often i have plucked you from my head
made with your smile a feast on my lapel
thinking, only a shrub can smile
with these many flowers

lo you are this scented rose
this dancing in the wind
this bouquet of memories
your eyes adorned with colours
flutter like butterflies
fly me to distant thoughts

my heart always was filled with nectar
            and fear
it returns to me now
garlanded with dead roots
dead leaves and
these twisted arteries of pain

you multiply into green leaves
too green sometimes you are bile
you with your branches of moods, your
twigs and tongue when you break off
and there is nothing but broken
leaves, thorns, and this
transcendental ache

a bed of dying memories
gather about my roots, fall
without protest, without sound

being too decayed, being
a morsel stuck in a hole in the tooth

i lie upon them in infinite repose
browned, greyed and one sided
for death is my awakening
ache, my rod and comfort
they tell me i am nothing
but a man

osa

i will untie you slowly perhaps
loose you from this sadness
which forms you into a knot of mystery
hold the fine threads of your melancholy
in my hands
and watch the sun rise from darkness

many fine rays come together
and become us
many sprays, liberated from rising waves
fall with salted pain
into our body of water

we are two echoes
finding purpose in empty repetitions
two streams of crystalline grief
separated by a hill
and i listen to you become my sea
become this untameable tempest
i call a heart

you are the universe i cannot master
this unknown i lose, midway to searching

what loosens leaves from their branches
what loosens tears, flowing like a river
from their wellspring
hiding behind my vision of you

is it this cold of an ending to a year
is it this bitterness of dying dreams
is it the sad plop plops that become a dirge
possessing your voice
darkening our eyes

a song comes to the end of melody
and becomes a sigh

a hem, i gather to my soul
spatters of your clinging mud

volcanoes open the twin gates of your eyes
they mist, flow over, flow
into this voice i listen to
run a path of molten words
you harden into silence
your tremblings seize me

      what pain knots you into this ball
      of tremblings
        what pain, what pain my poplar, what pain

i repeat myself with vain reflections
i repeat like the rain your salted sorrow

you open your mouth
and a conversation with silence follows
i open my mouth and i swallow it all
and in the well of those words, a deep
        and bottomless well
i drown myself, lost in the muck,
feet entangled, stuck
in the dark
        mesmerising miasma
           of your soul

and milestones

timi

soon, soon my brother, your songs too will take root
filled with spirit and glory
they will flourish as the nunswept breeze
that shakes by their roots our slumber

timi

you draw us to your courtyard
with a buff of polished parables
and your smile of seasons and
                enchantments
lures like the nun, tribal mark
across your face, filled
with riches and promise

your heart is the peerless moon
which illuminates our dark corners,
lights the path we walk with you
and we gather, each with his book
of tales, each with his bible of
petitions, each with his basket
of fruits and spices, planting dreams
into the wind that brings the night to sounds

sometimes the night is long, like a sad face
stretching far over many rivers
she covers our branches and gives light
to the eyes of owls, bats that darken
our forest of dreams

sometimes her chatter is a murmur of terror
like hyenas poised to pounce on the dying
sometimes her breath is the sound of hope gasping
but always your voice sings through
carries farther than the moon, farther
than growls crouching behind coiffured hair

you are as the palm a nation of gifts
and hold as wine song and anthem
you hold in your eyes the light of a people
their long suffering and mute yearnings
and we hold as the soil plants of flowering dreams

parched of earth we will the breeze to rise,

the trees to shake, her leaves to fall,
we will our will to take hold of air and rise
the rain to fall, the soil of our heart to grow tender
our plants to sprout, their roots to hold firm
with their many searching fingers
and nourish our famished earth

soon, soon my brother, your songs too will take root
filled with spirit and glory
they will flourish as the nunswept breeze
that shakes by their roots our slumber

they will flourish, you will flourish
we will flourish with you, flagstaff, canoehead
my brother
flourish as the sun that gives fire to our waters

a poet's hand
to chimanga

best western
allen
night

i sit at dinner
alone
pen and paper in hand
cutlery for a poet

outside is dark
once more

all around me
men, women eat
and chatter
and i, lost in words
lost in my world
eat the bits and pieces
of my mind

my dinner is
bitter
sweet
sour
all together me

as usual
nothing a la carte